D1528829

THE COLONIAL
CONQUEST OF ASIA

THE COLONIAL CONQUEST OF ASIA
BY JOHN G. ROBERTS

AN !MPACT BOOK

FRANKLIN WATTS | NEW YORK | LONDON | 1976

Photographs courtesy of: The Metropolitan Museum of Art: pp. 5, 6; Museum Nacional De Arte Antiga: p. 11; National Portrait Gallery: pp. 14, 21; New York Public Library Picture Collection: pp. 24 (top), 24 (bottom), 37; Philadelphia Museum of Art (A. J. Wyatt, staff photographer): p. 27; The Library of Congress: pp. 34, 38, 42, 53, 69; U.S. Navy: p. 45; United Press International: p. 60; U.S. Army: p. 66; The National Archives: p. 72; Information Service of India: p. 77.

Library of Congress Cataloging in Publication Data

Roberts, John G
    The colonial conquest of Asia.

    (An Impact book)
    Includes index.
    SUMMARY: Traces the history of the European and American colonization of South and East Asia from the first Portuguese explorers in the sixteenth century through the Vietnam War.
    1. Colonies in Asia—Juvenile literature. 2. Asia—History—Juvenile literature. 3. Imperialism—Juvenile literature. [1. Colonies in Asia. 2. Asia—History. 3. Imperialism] I. Title.
DS33.1.R6   325'.34'095   75–38615
ISBN 0–531–01126–7

CONTENTS

76 - 50

THE COLONIAL CONQUEST OF ASIA

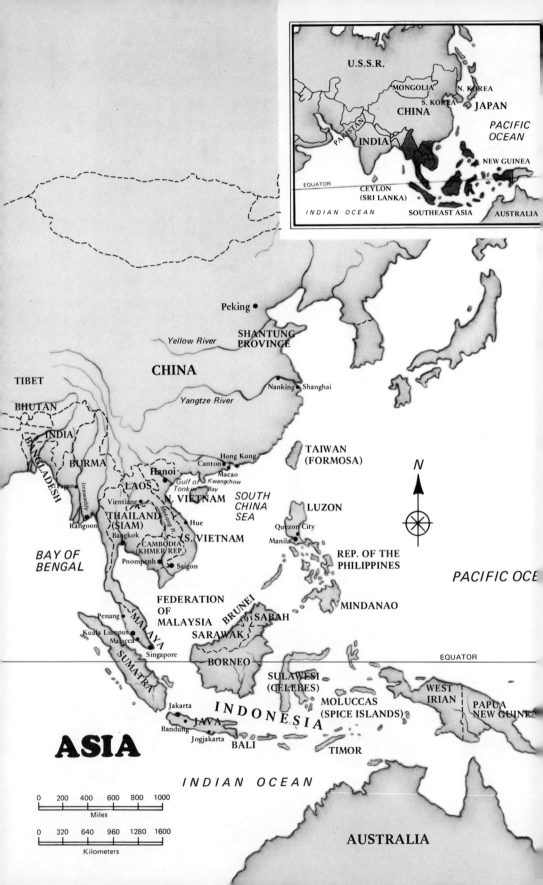

U.S.S.R.

MONGOLIA   N. KOREA
          S. KOREA
CHINA   JAPAN

PAKISTAN   PACIFIC
          INDIA   OCEAN

                                        NEW GUINEA

EQUATOR
          CEYLON
          (SRI LANKA)
INDIAN OCEAN   SOUTHEAST ASIA   AUSTRALIA

Peking

Yellow River   SHANTUNG
                      PROVINCE

CHINA

TIBET

BHUTAN
                              Nanking   Shanghai
INDIA   Yangtze River

BURMA   Hong Kong   TAIWAN
BANGLADESH   Canton   (FORMOSA)
          Pagana   Macao
          Irrawaddy   Hanoi   Kwangchow
                    LAOS   Gulf of   Bay
          Vientiane   Tonkin   SOUTH
                    N. VIETNAM   CHINA   LUZON
THAILAND   SEA
Rangoon   (SIAM)   Hue   Quezon City
          Bangkok   S. VIETNAM   Manila
                CAMBODIA
                (KHMER REP.)   REP. OF THE
          Pnompenh   Saigon   PHILIPPINES
BAY OF
BENGAL   MINDANAO
                    FEDERATION   BRUNEI
                    OF   SABAH
          Penang   MALAYSIA
          MALAYA   SARAWAK
Kuala Lumpur
     Malacca
          Singapore   BORNEO   EQUATOR
     SUMATRA
                                        SULAWESI
                                        (CELEBES)   WEST   PAPUA
                              MOLUCCAS   IRIAN   NEW GUINEA
          Jakarta   INDONESIA   (SPICE ISLANDS)
ASIA   JAVA
     Bandung   Jogjakarta   BALI
                    TIMOR

PACIFIC OCE

N

INDIAN OCEAN

0   200 400 600 800 1000
          Miles

0   320 640 960 1280 1600
          Kilometers

AUSTRALIA

CHAPTER 1
EAST MEETS WEST

The forcible conquest and domination of one nation by another has occurred in most inhabited regions of the globe. In fact, conquest has been a major influence in shaping the world. Invasions have fostered commerce, exchange of knowledge, adoption of better methods of production, the blending of different cultures and beliefs, and other benefits. Invasions have also disrupted life in conquered countries, debased cultures, and even destroyed civilizations.

In ancient Asia, extensive and relatively stable empires led to the development of cultures that excelled in the arts, philosophy, science, engineering, medicine, and social organization. Many important inventions such as movable type for printing, gunpowder, and the magnetic compass originated in Asia. All of the major religions practiced today began in Asia.

But civilizations are affected by many factors and do not develop evenly. During the fourteenth, fifteenth, and sixteenth centuries—the Renaissance—when the nations of Europe were rapidly developing their science and industry, the once-great Asian nations were declining. It was then that young, vigorous European nations began making voyages of discovery that would soon girdle the globe with new empires.

The word *Asia* means "Region of the Rising Sun." It was first used by the ancient Greeks, who traveled east to reach the vast continent. The region is also called the Orient —another word meaning "East." The area with which we are mainly concerned in this book is commonly called the

Far East. It may be divided into three parts: South Asia (India, Pakistan, Sri Lanka [formerly Ceylon], Bangladesh); Southeast Asia (the mainland territories of Burma, Thailand, Cambodia, Laos, Vietnam, and the Malay Peninsula, as well as the chains of islands upon which the nations of Indonesia and the Philippines are situated); East Asia (China and the Korean peninsula, the Japanese archipelago, eastern Siberia, and Sakhalin Island).

European nations subjugated nearly all the countries on or around Asia's southern and eastern shores. The mineral, agricultural, and human wealth of these countries was exploited to add to the prosperity and power of nations such as Portugal, Spain, Britain, France, the Netherlands, and later, the United States and Germany.

European conquerors brought modern communication, transportation, health care, and education to the lands they conquered. The improvements made the new lands more comfortable for the foreigners who came to live, made the land more productive, made it easier to get goods to market, and created a small, educated, native middle class to assist the foreigners. But essentially, improvements were intended to benefit local people only to the extent that they made them more useful.

Establishing control over a less developed land and people for purposes of trade, prestige, or power is called "imperialism." The people who dominate are called "imperialists." The so-called age of imperialism in Asia ended suddenly in the decades following the Second World War. But the ill effects of centuries of foreign domination in Asia have been profound and have not been fully overcome. To understand what is happening today in this populous and increasingly important region of the world, we must learn something of its tragic history.

Deep down inside, most people believe that their own families, friends, and countrymen are the best people in the world, and that their own schools, towns, states, and nations are superior to others. The Europeans who set out on the voyages of discovery thought themselves better than the people they encountered during their travels.

Prejudice, of course, was nothing new in Asia. The Chinese, for example, had long considered themselves superior to people from beyond their realm. All outsiders—including Europeans—were labeled barbarians. The proud Chinese felt they had nothing to learn from outsiders, and that the world should learn civilization and culture from them.

The European era of discovery changed both the scope of prejudice and its uses. On a worldwide scale, human differences became justification for violent conquest, economic exploitation, and cruelty. To justify such treatment, Europeans called the newly conquered people infidels or heathens—not Christian—refusing to admit that the Asians were heir to long-standing traditions of their own.

The people of the East were, in fact, not Christian. However, they practiced other religions. Hinduism became important in large areas of northern India, but attracted its largest number of followers in the south. The religion was already being practiced when, five hundred years before Christ, Gautama Buddha founded a religion that spread rapidly through India, China, and other parts of Asia. In the year A.D. 1000 northern India was conquered by Muslims—followers of the prophet Mohammed—from Central Asia. The Muslim faith, called Islam, flowered in northern India and won a tremendous following in other parts of Asia. Japan practiced both Buddhism and the Shinto religion. In China, Buddhism and Islam coexisted with Taoism, a kind of nature worship.

In Asia, the newcomers were encountering civilizations that had been in existence for at least five thousand years. China and India had well-developed cultures as old as those of Babylon, Egypt, and Persia. Ancient Greece and Rome, which reached the peak of their glory in the centuries just before and after the birth of Christ, were upstarts by comparison.

[3]

As early as 500 B.C. the Chinese had established a unified and rationally organized feudal system. But within a century it began to collapse. Wars among China's hundred states continued for 250 years. At the end of this era the emperor ordered the construction of the Great Wall, eventually 1400 miles long, as a defense against invasions by warlike nomads from the north. Parts of the wall still stand as proof of Chinese engineering and organizational skill. Still, the Great Wall did not keep out conquerors.

THE MOST EXTENSIVE ASIAN EMPIRE

The most brilliant of the Mongols—called Tartars by the Europeans—was Genghis Khan. In the thirteenth century he captured northern China, Turkestan, and Afghanistan. His mounted warriors were invincible because of their superb horsemanship and clever tactics of encirclement—learned from their main occupation, hunting. Genghis Khan carried his merciless campaigns as far as Persia and Russia. Under his successors, the Mongols probed westward all the way to Hungary, Poland, and the Balkans. His grandson, Kublai Khan, defeated the last of his Chinese opponents in 1279 and united China, Mongolia, and Korea.

The Mongols were driven out of China within a hundred years. But under Tamerlane, a descendant of Genghis Khan, they swept across South and West Asia, overwhelming the Russians in Turkestan and waging war in India

A tenth-century statue of the Indian god Brahma, the creator. His four heads and four arms represent his superhuman powers and his universality. The god is holding a string of prayer beads and a lotus flower, symbol of purity.

Akbar riding an elephant, a
painting done by a Mogul artist
in the early seventeenth century

and Asia Minor as well. Tamerlane was ruthless toward conquered peoples, including fellow Muslims. Upon taking a city, he would order his men to slaughter all the inhabitants and build pyramids from their skulls. One of Tamerlane's descendants, Babur, seized control over a large part of northern India. Babur's grandson Akbar became emperor of India in the sixteenth century. At the same time Elizabeth I reigned over the tiny kingdom of England.

During Elizabeth's reign East Asia was still a land of mystery to Europeans, but it was not entirely unknown. Quite a few of them had made the long journey overland to Cathay, as China was called, during the century when it was under Mongol rule. Ordinarily, overland communication between Europe and East Asia was difficult and hazardous. But Kublai Khan encouraged commerce and transportation, and people of different religions were tolerated. Thus, it was possible for Catholic missionaries and Christian, Jewish, and Muslim merchants as well as diplomats from Europe and Asia Minor to travel safely across the vast Mongol Empire. The empire extended from Europe and Persia to the Pacific Ocean. Merchants brought with them slaves, weapons, furs, and gems prized by wealthy Chinese. These goods were exchanged for silks, spices, perfumes, and medicinal plants, which could be sold in Europe at a high profit.

The best known of these early travelers was Marco Polo. At the age of seventeen he accompanied his father and uncle on an epic journey from their native Venice to China. Following the ancient Silk Route across Central Asia south of the Gobi Desert, their caravan reached the Great Wall and the Yellow River. After about four years' traveling, they reached the magnificent double-walled city of Cambaluc— later called Peking. The city was the capital of the Great Khan's empire. The visitors were also deeply impressed with his summer residence at Xanadu.

Marco served the Khan for seventeen years before returning to Venice by way of Sumatra, India, and Persia.

For centuries thereafter his book about his travels, *Description of the World,* was the main source of European knowledge about China and the East. The book proved useful to later explorers.

CHAPTER 2
HALF A WORLD WON—AND LOST

The voyages of discovery were perhaps the most daring exploits of the Renaissance. They greatly expanded the Western world's horizons and provided new wealth for its development. The motives for these dangerous and costly voyages across uncharted seas varied. Among them were curiosity, a yearning for wealth, power, or glory, and an urge to spread the Christian gospel.

Each man had his own reasons for risking his life to seek unknown lands, but all the voyages had one common purpose—trade. Through trade the kingdoms of Europe could get money to pay for frequent and costly wars. Through trade, the upper classes could get gems, rugs, rich fabrics, perfumes, spices, medicines, and art objects, the finest of which came from the Orient.

Muslim merchants controlled the sea routes to South Asia, and non-Christians of West and Central Asia monopolized overland transport and trade. Most cargo from the Orient was shipped across the Mediterranean to Venice for distribution to the rest of Europe. Venetians prospered, but other Europeans were becoming impatient to establish direct trade with the Orient.

Most active in seeking an alternate route to the East were the Portuguese, who had a long tradition of seafaring. They, like many Europeans, believed that somewhere in Asia or Africa there was a fabulously wealthy land ruled by a Christian monarch named Prester John. He would provide the courts of Europe with gold and also help them fight against the infidels—the Moors, Arab-Berber Muslims who had been at war with Europeans for centuries.

The Portuguese believed the mythical kingdom of Prester John was somewhere in Africa. They ventured farther and farther south along the African coast to find it. In 1488, Bartholomeu Dias reached the southernmost point of Africa, the Cape of Good Hope, proving that it was possible to reach the Indian Ocean from Portugal by sea. Another Portuguese, Vasco da Gama, at last opened the way to the Orient. Setting out in 1497, he rounded the Cape of Good Hope and sailed across the Indian Ocean to Calicut on the west coast of India.

As the sixteenth century dawned, Portugal was ready to stake out an empire that would span half the world. Under an agreement approved by the pope, Portugal and Spain were to divide all the non-Christian territories of the world between them. Portugal was awarded the Eastern Hemisphere, which included Asia.

THE POWER
OF PORTUGAL

Portuguese trade with India was developed to some extent by da Gama and his friend Pedro Alvarez Cabral. But the newcomers made enemies because of their harshness, and they were fiercely resisted by the Muslim traders who had long dominated commerce. In 1509 the warlike Francisco de Almeida, viceroy of Portuguese India, changed all that. With only a small fleet at his command, he defeated a Muslim armada of one hundred ships and assured Portuguese mastery of the Indian Ocean for a century thereafter.

Succeeding Almeida as viceroy was Alfonso d'Albu-

Prince Henry the Navigator.
This Portuguese prince improved
the compass and shipbuilding
and spent his life directing
voyages of discovery.

querque. With relentless ferocity he conquered or slaughtered adversaries and extended Portuguese control from the Persian Gulf eastward to the Straits of Malacca. This put the Portuguese in possession of the gateway from the Indian Ocean to Southeast Asia and the China Sea. Under Albuquerque's aggressive leadership, they strengthened their grip on Ceylon and penetrated Siam as well as the Moluccas—called the Spice Islands. Establishing a port at Macao, near today's Hong Kong, they conducted a brisk trade with China and Japan and virtually monopolized seagoing trade between Asia and Europe.

One exception to Portuguese supremacy in the East was the Philippine Islands. They had been claimed for the Spanish Crown by Ferdinand Magellan. He called there after having found the long-sought westward passage from Europe to the Orient by sailing around the tip of South America. Magellan was killed in the Philippines while trying forcibly to convert the local people to Christianity. Later on, his zeal was rewarded when the Philippines, under Spanish rule, became the only Christian country in Asia.

Early in the sixteenth century, the Portuguese city of Lisbon overtook Venice as the European market center for Oriental products. Lisbon's colonial trade was a monopoly of Portugal's royal house, which relied largely on foreign merchants to distribute the products in Europe.

The period of Portuguese control was already ending. In the colonies, Portuguese officials often neglected their duties or used their positions for personal gain. There were constant losses in wealth and manpower from wars, piracy, and shipwrecks. As Portugal's troubles multiplied, its Oriental outposts were steadily usurped by more vigorous Dutch and English colonizers.

Portugal's misfortunes accompanied the decline of the Holy Roman Empire, a confederation of Roman Catholic states that had dominated Europe for many centuries. During the Renaissance the countries of that empire, allied with staunchly Catholic Spain and Portugal, were trying desperately to resist political and economic changes. The Protestant Reformation in Northern Europe strengthened the nations opposing the political power of Rome. In the 1500s the Holy Roman Empire was weakened by a series of wars against the northern European Protestants, and also against Turkish Muslims who had invaded Central Europe. Taking advantage of the Holy Roman Empire's weakness, England and Holland began to challenge the Portuguese and Spanish monopoly of colonial trade.

THE ENGLISH AND DUTCH TAKEOVER

By the seventeenth century England had become quite prosperous. London was a commercial center, and merchants were looking for new markets and sources of goods. They had been keenly interested in the overseas exploits of Spain and Portugal but afraid to antagonize them by direct competition. The English served at first as middlemen for colonial products purchased in Spain and Portugal. The Dutch, under Spanish rule at that time, made similar arrangements, and Amsterdam too became an important trading port.

As English and Dutch explorers tried in vain to find new trade routes to the East Indies, merchants of those countries practiced widespread smuggling in Europe to bypass the Iberian monopolies. At the same time, English and French sea rovers raided Spain's and Portugal's fleets and confiscated their cargoes. (It was from such booty that England and France had learned of the great value of colonial trade.)

The most daring marauder was Francis Drake. A former slave-ship captain, Drake plundered Spanish treasure ships along the Spanish Main in Central America. On his most famous voyage he passed through the Strait of Magellan and, after raiding Spanish ships along the Pacific coast of the Americas, crossed the Pacific to the Spice Islands. Drake won exclusive trading rights there and was

Habes Lector candide fortiss. ac inuictiss. Ducis Draeck ad viuum Imaginem qui toto terrarum orbe, duorum annorum, et mensium decem spatio, Zephiris fauen: tibus circumducto, Anglium sedes proprias, 4. Cal Octobr. anno á partu Virgi: nis 1580 reuisit cum antea portu soluisset Id. Decem: anni. 1577.

also received favorably in the Celebes and Java. Having found a route that gave England unhindered access to the East Indies, he returned to Plymouth in 1580. He was the first Englishman to sail around the world.

In the same year, the king of Spain assumed control of Portugal. As a result, the English and Dutch merchants lost their profitable trading concessions in Lisbon. They redoubled their efforts to develop direct trade with the Orient.

The Dutch won Queen Elizabeth's support in their struggle for independence from Spain. Hostility between England and Spain blazed openly and ended in 1588 with the defeat of the Spanish Armada—a blow from which Spain never recovered.

England had already begun trading with the Philippines, Spain's colony, and soon took over the Portuguese slave trade in Africa. The Dutch, using secret information stolen from the Portuguese, had been making successful expeditions to Southeast Asia, and in 1602 they formed the Dutch East India Company to handle the trade. Two years previously Queen Elizabeth had permitted some London merchants to start an English company for the same purpose.

The two rival companies were authorized to maintain private armies, make and enforce laws, and coin money, as well as to conduct shipping and trade. The Dutch East India Company got a solid foothold in India, Ceylon, Java, Sumatra, and the Spice Islands. By taking over Malacca in 1641, the Dutch increased their power in the South China Sea and obtained a profitable monopoly on trade with Japan, which had closed its doors to all other Western countries. At the peak of its power, around 1670, the Dutch company owned more than 200 vessels and maintained an army of 10,000 soldiers in Asia.

The British East India Company, frozen out of other

Sir Francis Drake

regions of Asia by the Dutch, turned its attention to India, which proved to be an extremely valuable prize.

Before many decades had passed, the Dutch and English gained unchallenged supremacy in colonial Asia. Although their relative positions changed gradually, they remained the leading colonial powers there for the next three hundred years.

Spain held on to the Philippines, and Portugal retained a few bases such as Goa, Macao, and Timor while conducting a brisk trade among Asian seaports.

CHAPTER 3
THE BRITISH IN INDIA

The largest colonial possession in Asia was the British Indian Empire. At its peak it included India—the huge triangle of land jutting out from the Asian continent—Burma, and the island of Ceylon. By 1800, when the British East India Company had brought most of the region under its control, India had a population estimated at 200 million, far greater than the combined population of all the European countries including the Russian Empire.

The British got a late start in Asia. It was not until 1612, more than a century after Vasco da Gama's first voyage to the Indian city Calicut, that the East India Company won trading rights in India. After defeating one of Portugal's fleets, England established a base at the city of Surat. At the time, the Mogul—Indian Muslim—Empire, occupying a large part of North India, was ruled by Jahangir, a descendant of the Mongol conqueror Tamerlane. Under the Mogul emperors Europeans had been allowed to trade peaceably, as a rule. They were greatly impressed by the luxurious splendor of the courts of Indian princes.

Jahangir's son Shah Jahan, like his father, encouraged the arts, and was responsible for building the Taj Mahal as well as the Pearl Mosque at Agra. However, Shah Jahan was indifferent to the welfare of his people, and as a fanatical Muslim he treated the Hindus harshly. He was also intolerant of the Portuguese, who were already losing their grip on India. But he was friendly toward the English, and in 1639 he granted one of them the site upon which the city of Madras was founded.

Under the reign of Shah Jahan's son, the despotic Aurangzeb, there began a series of wars between Muslims and Hindus. The British East India Company's positions were endangered by both Aurangzeb and his enemies. The company representatives had learned to handle Indian rulers by alternately offering them military assistance and making threats. By such strategy the company retained its bases at Surat and Madras and also acquired, at little cost, the island of Bombay—formerly held by Portugal. Bombay, with the finest harbor in western India, became the company's regional headquarters.

A new and dangerous rival, the newly formed French East India Company, had appeared on the Indian scene. Winning the favor of the emperor, the French were permitted to establish commercial settlements at two cities, Pondicherry and Chandernagore. The latter city was close to the site of Calcutta, which was founded by the English in 1690, and became a focus of the Anglo-French disputes that followed.

In 1707, England, Wales, and Scotland united to create Great Britain. In the same year, with the death of Aurangzeb, the Mogul Empire disintegrated into a conglomeration of quarrelsome states. The following century of almost complete anarchy gave the foreign traders a chance to seize richer spoils. The rival East India companies curried favor with local princes and pitted one against the other in order to win more concessions.

By the middle of the eighteenth century the British East India Company was the largest and strongest enterprise in the world. Meanwhile, its Dutch rival had declined considerably.

ROBERT CLIVE

The most famous personage in the history of the British East India Company (and perhaps the most infamous) was Robert Clive, an Englishman who was employed by the firm at the age of eighteen. Clive had been an exceptionally poor student, and when sent out to Madras as a clerk he proved unruly and sometimes violent. With the outbreak of war between private armies of the French and British East India companies he showed talent as a soldier.

When the French commander captured Madras from the British in 1746, Clive was taken prisoner. Later, he escaped, rejoined the British forces, and was promoted to the rank of ensign. After the British regained Madras by treaty, the young officer was appointed to supply provisions to the troops. He used this opportunity to amass a fortune at the expense of his employers.

Hostilities were renewed when the French, by means of intrigue with local rulers, gained control over a large part of South India. In the decisive battle of Arcot, Clive used clever guerrilla tactics to rout the French army and reestablish British control over the southern territories.

Meanwhile, Calcutta, in the northern province of Bengal, had become the British company's most valuable trading center. The British had been on good terms with the ruler of Bengal, but when the company insisted upon fortifying Calcutta against his wishes, the Indian ruler's forces captured a company fort. Many British residents were imprisoned in the so-called Black Hole of Calcutta. Dozens died of wounds or suffocation.

Clive, now a lieutenant colonel, was given command of a large relief expedition. Transported by British warships, his troops rescued the surviving prisoners and recaptured Calcutta. Clive imposed harsh surrender terms on the defeated ruler. Clive forced him to pay a heavy indemnity (compensation for loss or damages) and gained permission for the company to fortify Calcutta.

By this time the Seven Years' War, in which France was pitted against Britain, had broken out. Using the war as an excuse, Clive seized the French trading center at Chandernagore in Bengal. Then, in a conspiracy with Hindu bankers and military leaders, he ousted the hostile ruler and installed a puppet of his own choice. This treachery enabled Clive to become the uncontested master of Bengal, India's richest province. In the course of these internal and external wars the British had almost expelled the Dutch and Portuguese from India. The Portuguese now held only a few isolated trading posts.

While Clive governed Bengal he persuaded the ruler to exempt his company's cargoes from the payment of duties. Goods handled by individual company members were also made duty free. This enabled individuals to enrich themselves by private trade. Not overlooking his own interests, Clive squeezed more than 200,000 pounds sterling from the Bengal government and acquired a valuable plantation as well as a Mogul title of nobility.

By encouraging religious and regional wars, the British East India Company kept India in continuous disorder. Serving a second term as governor of Bengal, Clive forced the powerless Mogul emperor to give the company the right to collect taxes in two rich states and the right to exercise police and judicial powers. Under Clive there was a great famine (1769–1770) in Bengal, due in part to British disruption of the economy. During the famine Clive insisted upon collecting the full tax revenue for the company even though about one-third of the population was starving to death.

When Robert Clive returned to England a rich man, he was made a baron, knighted, and became a member of Parliament.

The British East India Company's relentless expansion made South Asia a reservoir of agricultural and mineral products—cotton, hemp, silk, indigo, sugar, spices, tea, coffee, opium, and saltpeter for gunpowder, among others—produced by some of the cheapest labor in the world. And despite the poverty of its millions of people,

Robert Clive

India became a valuable market for goods manufactured in England.

On the other hand products manufactured in India, mainly textiles, were largely excluded from England by high tariffs. Handmade Indian fabrics had become tremendously popular with British ladies, so to stifle competition the British East India Company broke up Indian handicraft industries. The skilled craftsmen were forced onto the overcrowded farms, where the lion's share of the produce was appropriated by absentee landlords.

Under the monoculture system (cultivation of one product) fostered by the British, Indian farmers were forced to produce export commodities, while the growing of food for the local population was neglected. The result in India was higher prices for food (because of scarcity) and appalling famines.

Sharing responsibility for the plunder and destruction in India were twenty-four Englishmen acting for the company's two thousand stockholders. These owners, some of whose descendants are still among the wealthiest people in the United Kingdom, managed to control whole countries and their teeming millions with little help from the British government except in time of war. When Clive was at the peak of his power, the European colonists and their families were protected by only about 20,000 British and European troops—one soldier for every 100,000 Indians. The imperialists left most of the fighting and policing to the *sepoys,* Indian soldiers, who at all times outnumbered the foreign troops by at least five to one.

THE SEPOY REBELLION

Sepoys were easily recruited. Most other careers were closed to Indians. They were strictly disciplined to follow orders from their British officers. Many of these native policemen were Nepalese Gurkhas (Hindus descended from the Mongols) and long-bearded Sikhs from the Punjab. They were professional killers and feared by the local people even more than the British, who left the more barbarous acts of bloodshed to them.

The arrogance, brutality, and corruption of the white rulers, known collectively as the British *raj,* aroused concern and indignation among some Englishmen at home. Finally, in 1784, Parliament made the British East India Company responsible to a board of control appointed by the crown and gave a governor general the power to supervise its activities. After that, there was gradual improvement in some aspects of Indian life, such as transportation, administration, and education. English was introduced as the official language, the company's monopoly of trade was abolished, and Christian evangelists were allowed to do missionary work in territories controlled by the company. But these reforms were made more for the stability of the British raj than for the advancement of the people. As late as 1793, for example, when India's judicial system was reshaped after the British system, Indians were excluded from high positions such as district judgeships.

Resistance to British power blazed openly in the Sepoy Rebellion of 1857–58. The causes were various, involving religious superstitions, cultural friction, and confiscations of land. The Bengalese sepoys mutinied first. Sepoys all over northern and central India followed. Hindu and Muslim rulers besieged Lucknow and captured Cawnpore as well as Delhi, where they proclaimed the Mogul emperor sovereign of all India.

Most of the rebel leaders rallied to the emperor's side, but some of the largest sepoy units remained loyal to the British. During the mutiny in Cawnpore, more than two hundred British women and children were massacred. This act was used as a pretext for drastic suppression when the British recaptured the three cities after months of guerrilla warfare. Delhi was sacked and its remaining inhabitants massacred. The emperor, last of the Moguls, was deposed and exiled.

This victory was the company's last one. In 1858, Parliament passed the Government of India Act under

which administration was transferred to the British crown. The East India Company no longer served any useful purpose. Queen Victoria proclaimed a new policy under which the British would cease annexing lands and interfering in religious matters. Minor positions in the civil service were opened to qualified Indians. Thereafter, reforms of the legal system enabled the conquerors to rule India with less violence, and serious attempts were made to encourage social development on the British pattern.

In 1877, Victoria was proclaimed empress of India, and the native princes were solemnly assembled at Delhi to offer homage. Pehaps they were inspired, as were the more sentimental British, by Victoria's statement of policy. She declared, "We hold ourselves bound to the natives of our Indian territories by the same obligations of duty which bind us to our other subjects." At that very time, whether the queen knew it or not, five million of her new subjects were starving to death in a great famine that swept over southern India. In the six decades of British rule that followed the Sepoy Rebellion, the total number of Indians who died of starvation and epidemics probably exceeded the entire population of Victoria's "other subjects."

Top: *rescuing the British at Lucknow during the Sepoy Rebellion.* Bottom: *a British agent forcing an Indian merchant to give up his money. Reprisals such as this were said to be common after the Sepoy Rebellion.*

CHAPTER 4
A KEY TO THE CELESTIAL EMPIRE

From the fifteenth century onward European governments needed more and more money, mainly for war. The most widely accepted form of money in Europe was bullion—bars of gold or silver—and the most satisfactory way of getting it legally was through foreign commerce. The goal of this trade was expressed in the international balance-of-payments theory which held that a nation should have more gold or silver coming into the state treasury than going out. In practice this meant importing cheap raw materials and exporting expensive manufactured goods.

Governments held down imports of manufactured goods from the colonies and used their possessions as sources of raw materials that could be imported to Europe and turned into manufactured goods. (Imports were also held down from competing countries in Europe, and goods allowed in were heavily taxed.) In addition to keeping tight control over foreign markets, sources of raw materials, and monopolizing trade routes, the nations of Europe fought each other when necessary to protect their advantages. This policy, called mercantilism, was the general rule in Europe until about 1800.

Predictably, mercantilist policy fostered industry at the expense of agriculture. The great boost that mercantilism gave to manufacturing, science, and technology was known as the Industrial Revolution. It vastly increased the economic and military power of the countries in which it occurred most rapidly—Great Britain, France, the Netherlands, Germany, and the United States.

[26]

*A Chinese scholar's study,
late eighteenth century*

In the process of industrialization, the Western nations moved toward the modern form of industrial capitalism, in which private wealth and initiative became more important than in the old European system of government-protected trade monopolies. Individual profit through competition became a major social force. But businessmen still worked closely with the government in foreign activities that mirrored national ambitions.

In Asia, the Industrial Revolution had scarcely begun. In general, the ruling classes were interested mainly in preserving their traditional privileges, and, as in medieval Europe, they opposed social changes of any kind. Nearly everyone else lived from agriculture or handicrafts. Peasants knew little of the world outside the villages in which they spent their entire lives unless uprooted by war or famine. Isolated and neglected, they had little or no feeling of being part of a nation.

Most Asians were obedient to long-established customs and traditions and remained in the social position assigned to them at birth. The social and economic unit was the family, which included not only the parents and children but also grandparents, married sons and daughters, grandchildren, and other relatives. Agricultural methods were primitive, and manufacturing remained in a handicraft stage because village life was not suitable for division of labor and large-scale production. The traditional way of living had its pleasures and satisfactions—at least in times of peace and abundant harvests—and most people accepted it as the natural order of things.

Spurred on by the Industrial Revolution and the need for foreign markets and raw materials, European imperialists moved into the countries of Asia at an increasingly rapid pace. By the end of the eighteenth century, most regions of South and Southeast Asia had been claimed and were being divided up according to changes in the relative power of the conquerors.

The British East India Company had little trouble snatching Ceylon from the Dutch. The Dutch East India

Company, like the Portuguese before them, was greatly weakened by corruption, mismanagement, and the cost of military operations. However, the British let the Dutch keep Sumatra, Java, the Celebes, and most of Borneo. Spain was left undisturbed in the Philippines, and Portugal retained a part of Timor Island as well as its old colonies of Goa and Macao.

The British could afford such tolerance because they had become masters of the seas. Ousting the Dutch from Malacca, they established settlements which later became the Federated Malay States (now Malaysia), and began the gradual conquest of Burma. In 1819 a noted British colonial administrator, Sir Thomas Stamford Raffles, had founded Singapore on an island facing the Strait of Malacca. The port was developed into an impregnable naval base securing British access to East Asia.

Great Britain, having lost its most valuable colonies in the New World as a result of the American Revolution, had taken a keen interest in the markets of China and Japan. During the reign of the Ming dynasty (1368–1644), foreign countries had been permitted to trade with China, the Celestial Empire, if they acknowledged the supremacy of the emperor, called the Son of Heaven. Submissive rulers sent diplomatic missions at regular intervals to Peking, where they kowtowed (touching the forehead to the ground while kneeling) to the emperor and presented valuable gifts as tribute. In this way, extensive commerce had been developed between China and countries of East and Southeast Asia.

The Dutch and Portuguese submitted to the tribute system, and their ships called freely at Chinese ports. The British proudly refused. As a result their East India Company was permitted to trade only at Canton in southern China. Foreigners in Canton were hemmed in by rules and regulations intended to protect the Chinese people from foreign "contamination." Foreigners were not permitted to live in the city. They were confined to an area of warehouses and residences outside Canton's walls. They could not deal directly with Chinese merchants. All trade was handled through official agents, called *hong* merchants. The hong merchants (two men handled all the legal foreign traders in the 1880s) were not only responsible for seeing to it that trade was carried on smoothly, but were also responsible for the personal behavior of the foreigners assigned to them, and were punished when foreigners misbehaved. Over the years since 1685, when these rules were first instituted, many other restrictions were added. For example, foreigners could not bring their wives and could not associate with Chinese women. No Chinese could teach his language to a foreigner.

In spite of such difficulties, trade flourished at Canton. By the early 1880s the British were handling the largest share of China's foreign commerce. The British Canton trade was of two types: "country trade," or trade between China and other Asian countries, and trade between China and Great Britain. Country trade was conducted mainly by independent ship owners. This usually meant British officers commanding Indian or Chinese crews. The second type of trade was in the hands of the East India Company. The main cargo carried by the ships sailing between China and the mother country was tea. It had become Britain's national beverage and replaced silk as China's main export. As the British developed export products in India, the volume of country trade between India and China grew larger and more important as a source of silver bullion for England.

This country trade strengthened the company's monopoly in two important ways. Calling at many smaller ports, the privately owned ships established commercial contacts and pioneered new markets for products handled by the company. More important, they provided a means of paying for China's products without spending Britain's reserve of bullion.

The method was quite simple: the country traders brought India-made products to Canton and sold them to hong merchants for silver money. This they deposited with the East India Company at Canton. In exchange, the country traders received bills which they could exchange for hard money in Calcutta or London. In this roundabout way, most of China's tea and silk purchased by the British was paid for with silver obtained from China itself, by selling the Chinese goods produced in India.

China's main import from India was raw cotton. But rivaling it in value was opium, which was produced in India and sold by the company to country traders who transported it to Canton. This ingenious arrangement, begun for economic convenience, led to some of the most tragic episodes in modern history.

CHAPTER 5
THE POWER
OF OPIUM

Opium, made of juice obtained from the pods of certain poppies, had been used as medicine in India and China for a thousand years or more without causing problems. The smoking of opium, which is habit-forming, was not begun until the 1620s, when tobacco was introduced into China. At first, the opium was mixed with smoking tobacco, a practice said to have been learned from European traders. The harmful effects of opium smoking were soon recognized in China, and the import and sale of the drug were prohibited. Still, opium smoking became a pastime of the upper classes, who set an example for those less able to afford it. Although the drug was illegal, it was easy to get. The central government in Peking was decaying, and law enforcement elsewhere in the country had been undermined by corruption. Equally important, country traders and their Chinese accomplices were skillful smugglers.

Cultivated on a large scale in Bengal, opium was very cheap to produce. In China it brought high prices. In the 1830s country traders were smuggling some 40,000 chests —more than 5 million pounds—each year into China.

The supply of opium was monopolized by the British East India Company. The drug accounted for about one-fifth of the company's total earnings. Country traders received a license from the company that said they could use their vessels only for loading opium. Chinese officials took bribes and closed their eyes to the illegal trade.

Foreign merchants, though prosperous, became increasingly bitter about the conditions under which they had to live and do business outside Canton. The British government too was dissatisfied with the arrangement and wanted to establish diplomatic relations with the Chinese government so that a better trade relationship could be developed. The British wanted all of China opened to trade. The huge country would be a vast market for British and Indian goods. Already, British ships were calling at several of China's ports, but this was illegal. Other foreign countries involved in the Canton trade were also unhappy about the restrictions. China's rulers were under heavy pressure to make treaties that would permit trade on a more modern basis.

The British urged that opium imports be made legal. This would allow them to conduct lucrative business in a more orderly way, without the expense of bribery and the competition of smugglers. But China's government had discovered that the opium traffic, besides being harmful socially, was causing a serious drain of the silver bullion needed for legitimate trade and the operation of the monetary system. The rulers turned down the British proposal and decreed the death penalty for all producers, handlers, or users of opium.

An official was sent from Peking to smash the drug traffic in Canton itself. When the foreign traders refused to give up the opium in their possession, they were held captive in the warehouse area. After six weeks of confinement they handed over 20,000 chests of opium (worth $10 million) and were released. The opium was destroyed. The resulting scarcity of the drug caused the price to double. At $1,000 a chest the illegal trade continued.

This incident, and others involving the foreigners' refusal to submit to China's laws, resulted in the Opium War (1839–42), during which British easily defeated China's poorly armed, demoralized, opium-addicted troops. After seizing and occupying several major seaports and threatening Nanking, Britain forced China's tottering government to surrender.

On August 29, 1842, the Treaty of Nanking ended the

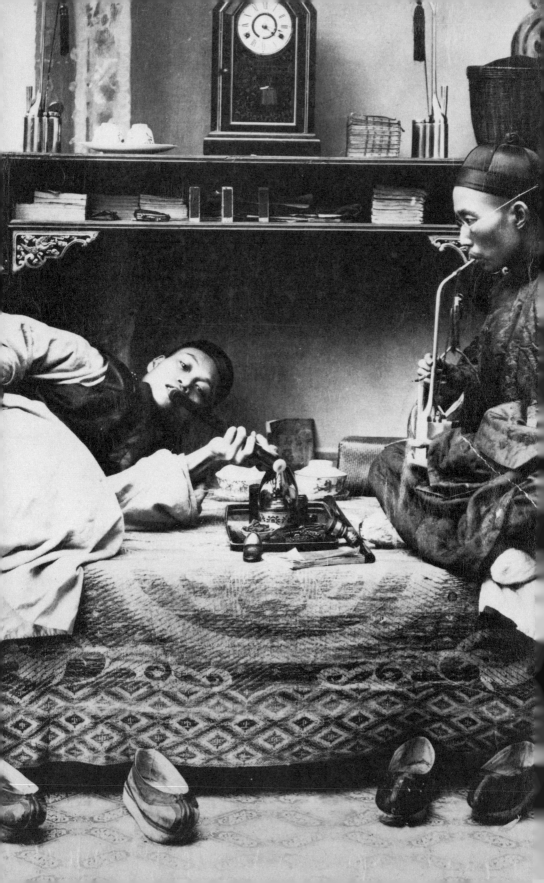

war, terminated the tribute system as well as the Canton monopoly over foreign trade, and opened up five ports, including Canton and Shanghai, to British trade under diplomatic protection. The island of Hong Kong, with a splendid harbor, was ceded to Great Britain, which also received an indemnity of 21 million pounds sterling. (Six million of this was payment for the destruction of the 20,000 chests of smuggled opium destroyed earlier.) Tariffs on imports were set at the low rate of about 5 percent. Under subsequent treaties, Britain was given most-favored-nation status. This meant Britain would automatically be granted all privileges given to other countries under treaties. The Nanking treaty also gave Christian missionaries special privileges to assist them in making converts. Nothing was said about stopping the drug trade.

Although the United States and France had not participated in the war, they stepped in to demand the same rights given to Britain and also obtained extraterritorial status for their citizens. This status, later given to all foreign residents, exempted them from trial in China's courts for any and all crimes. In China, the white man was above the law.

Under these so-called unequal treaties, foreigners set up thriving settlements in the open ports. Living securely in little worlds of their own, attended by poorly paid Chinese servants, they profited richly from the expansion of trade. Unfortunately, China's demand for Western manufactured goods grew slowly, so the British—as well as American, French, and other foreign merchants—continued to pay for their purchases with opium. As addiction to the drug increased, opium imports nearly doubled, and the weak central government could do nothing to stop the traffic. In some provinces nine out of ten Chinese men were opium addicts.

In the midst of troubles caused by internal decay,

Smoking opium

[35]

alien intrusion, and the humbling of the ruling dynasty, there was rising discontent among the people. Especially oppressed were the farmers, who were reduced to near starvation by taxes and exorbitant payments to landlords. Also, droughts and floods due to government neglect of irrigation systems and dams caused terrible famines. These grievances came to a focus in the Taiping Rebellion, 1850–64. The movement was based on a blend of Christianity, socialism, and nationalism. The Taiping rebels captured part of China and set up a rival government. In the area they controlled, the rebels began social reforms to benefit workers and peasants and women.

The British and French exploited the social upheaval to make new demands on China's government. As soon as the British had put down the sepoy mutiny in India, a force was sent to Canton and captured the walled city. When British and French envoys, backed by strong military forces, entered the city of Tientsin, government negotiators yielded new concessions. Under the treaties of Tientsin, which were granted in 1858 to the United States and Russia as well as to Great Britain and France, China opened eleven more ports to foreign trade. The treaties also permitted foreign powers to open legations (diplomatic missions headed by a minister) in Peking. And Christian missionaries were allowed in the interior of China. In subsequent negotiations, foreigners were given control over customs in the open ports, and finally the import of opium was made legal.

These terms were so harsh that the Manchu court refused to ratify the treaty, and in 1860 the British and French launched a massive campaign known as the Second Opium War. Peking was occupied by 17,000 foreign troops, and the emperor's ancient and magnificent Summer Palace, consisting of some two hundred buildings with priceless works of art, was looted by the invaders and put to the torch. By such means the foreign powers secured Chinese acceptance of the 1858 treaties plus new concessions. Britain was granted a lease on the Kowloon Peninsula opposite

*Weighing the money China
was forced to pay as indemnity
after the treaties of Tientsin*

Hong Kong. Catholic missions were allowed to own property inland. China was forced to pay increased indemnities. In the same year China ceded to the Russian Empire the extensive Maritime Territory east of Manchuria. There, the Russians founded a city, Vladivostok, as a base for further colonial penetration of Asia.

Having battered down the gates of the Celestial Empire and placed their ministers within the capital city, the foreign powers turned their attention to the rival Taiping government. British and French forces, aided by American-led Chinese mercenaries, and troops loyal to the central government, destroyed the rebels. Now the rulers of China, the Manchu, whose ancestors had come as conquerors centuries before, were at the mercy of new conquerors.

A pack train traveling the
rugged landscape of North China.
The Great Wall snakes across
the hills in the distance.

CHAPTER 6
JAPAN LEARNS THE GAME

Europeans began to arrive at Japanese ports in the middle of the sixteenth century. They were treated courteously and allowed to trade. Roman Catholic missionaries taught the gospel and made many converts including some powerful lords. Later in the century, however, the aggressiveness of the Spanish and Portuguese Catholic missionaries alarmed Japan's leaders, who suspected that they were being used as the entering wedge for the conquest of Japan. Foreign priests were executed or expelled, and their native converts severely persecuted. In one uprising in 1638 nearly 40,000 Japanese Christians were killed.

Soon thereafter, Japan's doors were closed to all but a trickle of foreign commerce. The Dutch, in part because they were Protestant, were allowed to trade at Nagasaki, in southwestern Japan. Relations with China continued. Chinese merchant ships called at Nagasaki as well as at the Ryukyu Islands, which were under both Japanese and Chinese influence. With these exceptions foreign vessels were forbidden to enter Japan's waters. Foreigners landing on Japan's soil faced the death penalty. The Japanese—skillful navigators in the past—were forbidden to build ships large enough for overseas voyages. They were prohibited also from leaving the country on foreign vessels. For more than two hundred years Japan lived like an oyster in its shell.

This era of isolation suddenly came to an end in 1854 when Commodore Matthew C. Perry, commanding a small fleet of U.S. Navy steamships, made his second expedition to Japan. On his first visit, the year before, he had de-

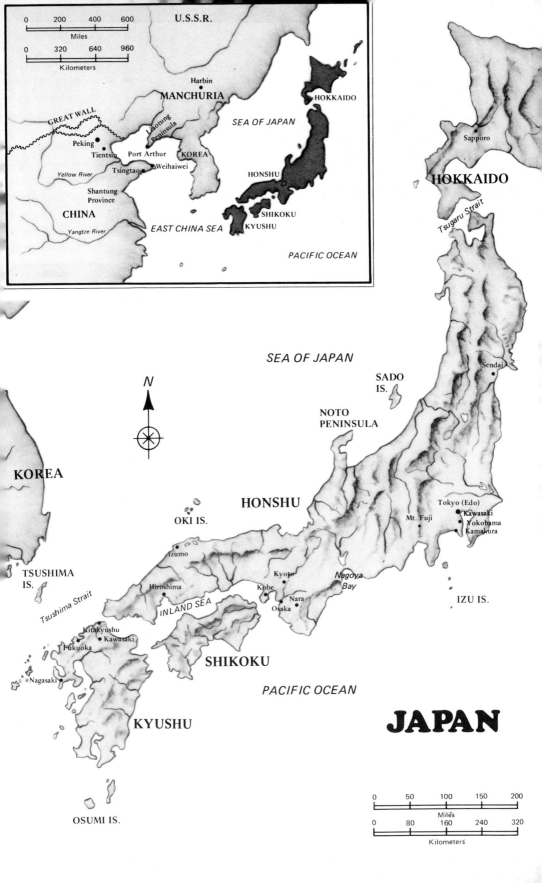

U.S.S.R.

Miles
0   200   400   600

Kilometers
0   320   640   960

MANCHURIA

Harbin

GREAT WALL

Liaotung Peninsula

Peking

Tientsin

KOREA

Port Arthur

Tsingtao

Weihaiwei

Yellow River

Shantung Province

CHINA

Yangtze River

EAST CHINA SEA

SEA OF JAPAN

HOKKAIDO

HONSHU

SHIKOKU

KYUSHU

PACIFIC OCEAN

HOKKAIDO

Sapporo

Tsugaru Strait

SEA OF JAPAN

Sendai

SADO IS.

NOTO PENINSULA

N

KOREA

HONSHU

OKI IS.

Izumo

Tokyo (Edo)

Kawasaki

Mt. Fuji

Yokohama

Kamakura

Kyoto

Nagoya Bay

Kobe

Nara

Osaka

IZU IS.

TSUSHIMA IS.

Tsushima Strait

Hiroshima

INLAND SEA

Kitakyushu

Kawasaki

Fukuoka

SHIKOKU

Nagasaki

PACIFIC OCEAN

KYUSHU

JAPAN

Miles
0   50   100   150   200

Kilometers
0   80   160   240   320

OSUMI IS.

manded that Japan open diplomatic relations with the United States. Now Perry sailed almost within gunshot of the city where the *shogun,* Japan's ruler, held court. The commodore refused to leave until the government signed a treaty. Perry dared to do this because Japan had no proper navy and no coastal defenses strong enough to drive him away.

The United States government had no desire to colonize Japan. America wanted Japan to allow U.S. whalers and merchant vessels that were active in the northern Pacific to take refuge in bad weather, make repairs, and obtain fuel, food, and water. The move was also political. The United States wanted to prevent Britain, who had already occupied many seaports in East Asia, from dominating the Pacific Ocean.

Japan had never opened diplomatic relations with any Western power and was in a quandary over what to do about Commodore Perry. The shogun's government understood its helplessness against the superior ships and guns and proposed to open the country to trade. More patriotic leaders opposed this course, demanding that the "barbarians" be ousted forcibly, regardless of the consequences.

After much wrangling, Japan yielded to Perry and signed a treaty. They hoped this would buy time for bolstering the nation's defenses. According to the terms of the treaty two minor ports were opened to foreign ships, which would be permitted to take on supplies. Shipwrecked American sailors were to be treated humanely. And finally, under a most-favored-nation clause, the United States was to be granted the same privileges given later to any other country.

The treaty did not give Americans the right to trade,

Commodore Matthew C. Perry, as drawn by a Japanese artist during the treaty negotiations that ended Japan's isolation from the West but it did allow them to post consuls in the open ports. The consul would live at the port and represent the United States in all matters regarding commerce. In 1857 Townsend Harris, a former merchant from New York, landed in Japan as the first diplomatic representative of a Western power. By persuasion, threats, and enormous patience he negotiated a second treaty which opened four more ports and allowed Americans to live in Japan's two largest cities, Edo—now Tokyo—and Osaka. As in China, the United States insisted that its citizens not be subject to the laws of Japan. Americans could not be tried in Japan's courts. The United States also reserved the right to set low import duties. In quick time Holland, Russia, Great Britain, and France signed similar unequal treaties with the shogun's government. A foreign seaport and settlement was established at Yokohama, near Edo, and trade developed rapidly.

Opium was strictly prohibited, but Japan was receptive to foreign manufactured goods. Unfortunately Japan did not have enough export products to exchange for imports, and as in China foreign trade caused a serious outflow of bullion. This drain was aggravated by the greed of foreign merchants, who took advantage of Japanese unfamiliarity with Western money matters and bought gold at a fraction of its actual value. This contributed to the collapse of Japan's outdated monetary system. There were other economic problems. The exports of necessary commodities caused prices in Japan to rise steeply. Imported manufactures competed so severely with locally made products that Japan's handicraft industries were nearly ruined.

Economic distress and the arrogant and unruly behavior of many foreigners aroused indignation among the proud Japanese. Antiforeign sentiment was particularly strong among the two-sworded *samurai*. This elite warrior class felt that the shogun had betrayed the nation by allowing foreigners to defile the land of the gods. Determined to drive the Western intruders out of Japan, they committed numerous acts of arson and violence in which for-

High-ranking Japanese receiving
gifts brought by Matthew Perry
as a gesture of friendship and a
display of Western technology. The
gifts included a miniature steam
locomotive. In the background, the
Americans have set up telegraph lines
to demonstrate rapid communication.

eign merchants and diplomatic employees were killed. Foreign governments retaliated by bombarding Japanese towns and imposing heavy indemnities on the shogun's government.

In the meantime, some of the younger samurai had swallowed their pride and visited European countries, where they discovered that Japan had fallen far behind in technical and military matters. One of them, Hirobumi Ito, in later years became Japan's first prime minister and most influential statesman. On his return from London, he warned that Japan had much to learn before it could hope to drive out the foreigners. Ito and some of his fellow samurai, still in their twenties and thirties, organized a national movement to overthrow the shogun—whose ancestors had usurped authority centuries ago—and to restore power to the ancient imperial house. With British help they trained and equipped armies of rebellious samurai to fight the shogun's far more numerous troops. After a brief war they captured Edo, the shogun's capital, renamed it Tokyo ("Eastern Capital"), and established the new imperial government there.

The restoration of the emperor, whose long reign is called the Meiji era, marked the beginning of Japan's modernization by a small group of samurai who entrenched themselves in power. In the name of Emperor Meiji, an absolute monarch, they united Japan's many clans under a strong central government. Their goal was expressed in the slogan, *A strong army in a rich country*. They reasoned that modern industry could provide wealth and military strength. To accomplish modernization they decided to create social and economic conditions similar to those in the most powerful Western countries.

In response to the challenge of the West, Japan did something that no other country had done; it revolutionized its social structure from top to bottom and proceeded deliberately and speedily to build a modern economy. Representatives were sent abroad to cultivate the arts of commerce and diplomacy. Students and observers accompanied them to learn Western ways of doing things. Foreign teachers and specialists were brought to Japan to educate and train the people. Compulsory education for both sexes was introduced to prepare young people for building the new Japan.

The first task was to increase Japan's economic and military power. Japan did not wait for the Industrial Revolution to occur gradually, as it had in the West through the private enterprise system. The government itself developed mines, arsenals, shipyards, and manufacturing industries, then later turned them over to private businessmen. In this way Japan reduced its dependence on foreign imports and became more self-sufficient.

Another important task of the Meiji government was to cancel the unequal treaties. To accomplish this, Japan's legal, commercial, and banking systems were revised along Western lines. The army was remodeled on the French pattern. The navy and the parliament were British-style, and a German-type code of laws was created. Japan's government officials and businessmen adopted Western-style clothing, hair styles, food, and etiquette. Such novelties, along with European literature, art, and music, became a craze with Japan's growing middle class.

Foreigners laughed at the imitativeness of the Japanese, not realizing its purpose. But in 1894 the British government finally agreed to a new treaty, effective within five years, abolishing the most objectionable features of the unequal treaties.

This was followed by similar agreements with other countries. It meant, for one thing, that Japan could now set import tariffs high enough to protect its own industries and obtain much-needed revenue for modernization.

Japan began to come under the same pressures that had driven European powers to seek colonies. The country was poor in natural resources and had to import raw materials needed for industry. For this reason, Japan felt a

PEOPLE'S REPUBLIC OF CHINA

MANCHURIA

U.S.S.

Tumen River

• Ch'ongjin

Hyesan •

Yalu River

Changjin R.

• Kanggye

NORTH

KOREA

• Kimchaek

Yalu River

• Sinuiju

Chongchon R.

Liaotung Peninsula

Hamhung •
Hungnam •

• Dairen
• Port Arthur

Taedong

Nam R.

• Wonsan

KOREA BAY

Namp'o • • Pyongyang

Imjin R.

SEA OF JAPAN

P'anmunjom •

Kaesong •

Seoul •

Pukhan R.

• Chunchon

• Kangnung

ULLUNG IS.

• Weihaiwei

Shantung
Province

Inchon •

Yungdungp'o •

• Suwon

• Samchok

• Wonju

Chungju •

Han

Chonan •

YELLOW SEA

• Andong

SOUTH

Kum R.

Taejon •

KOREA

Pohang-dong •

Kum R.

• Taegu

• Kyongju

Kunsan •

Choniu •

Kum R.

• Ulsan

Naktong

NORTH
AND
SOUTH
KOREA

Kwangju •

Chinju •

Masan •

Nam

Pusan •

Somjin R.

Mokpo •

Korea Strait

HUKSAN
IS.

CHEJU IS.

JAPAN

Kyush

0   50   100   150

Miles

0   80   160   240

Kilometers

strong urge to gain a foothold in Asian countries where minerals and other commodities were more abundant and where manufactured goods could be marketed.

Japan's first conquest was the Ryukyu Islands, the largest of which is Okinawa. These islands had been protected by China under the tributary system but through trade they were more closely linked with Japan. They were taken over in 1874, after a brief Japanese invasion of Formosa, a Chinese island.

For hundreds of years Japan had been trying to force its way into Korea. The land was called the Hermit Kingdom because, as a vassal of China, it avoided contact with any other country. The weakness of China made Korea more and more appealing to imperialist powers. Between 1866 and 1871, successive French, German, and American expeditions had invaded the country only to be driven out. In 1876 Japan, by threats and trickery, forced Korea's monarch to open three ports, establish diplomatic relations, and give Japanese subjects special privileges. This strategy, copied from the Western imperialists, gave Japan the chance to infiltrate secret agents, organize a pro-Japanese faction, and play the old game of divide and conquer.

From then on, Japan was engaged in a power struggle with China for control of Korea. In 1894, during an insurrection, the king of Korea asked China for help. Several thousand Chinese troops were dispatched. Japan, to protect its own position, then sent in twice as many soldiers and occupied Seoul, Korea's capital. A new dispute with China arose, and in the ensuing Sino-Japanese War (1894–95) Japan astonished the world by destroying China's navy and routing its armies. Suddenly, Japan became a power to be reckoned with.

The war was settled by a treaty under which China ceded to Japan the island of Formosa and the Liaotung Peninsula in southern Manchuria. In addition, China paid Japan an indemnity of about $150 million in silver. Having taken care to learn the rules of the game, Japan had not only escaped conquest by the imperialists, but had become an imperialist power itself. Now possessing colonies of its own as well as a privileged position in Korea, Japan also enjoyed diplomatic and commercial rights in China equal to those of the major Western powers.

But the rules of the game are made by those powerful enough to enforce them. When the rules work against the enforcers, they can be changed or ignored. Shortly after China signed the treaty, Russia, France, and Germany forced Japan to give up its claim to the Liaotung Peninsula. This so-called Triple Intervention humiliated the Japanese. They were further outraged when the Russian Empire took over the southern part of the peninsula with its strategic ports of Dairen and Port Arthur. From then on, Japan's ambition, already alarming to the Western powers, was reinforced by a thirst for revenge.

CHAPTER 7
THE AGE OF IMPERIALISM

The quickening tempo of conquest in Asia reflected changes that were occurring in Western countries toward the end of the nineteenth century. In simplest terms, the West had money and wanted profitable fields of investment. Those who owned or controlled capital found that profits were much higher in colonial areas than at home. There were many reasons for this: labor was cheap and docile, taxes low or nonexistent, and the regulation of commerce largely in the hands of the foreign businessmen themselves. Also, improvements in steamships and the completion of the Suez Canal in 1869 had made transportation between Europe and Asia much quicker and cheaper. By the 1880s a new phase of conquest, called the age of imperialism, had begun in earnest.

Nearly all of South and Southeast Asia already had been divided among the major colonial powers. The British took Burma—a country with plentiful rice, timber, and minerals—after the collapse of the Manchu government's authority in China. The French annexed or gained control over Cochin China, Annam, and Tonkin (the three regions that form today's Vietnam), as well as Cambodia and Laos, all of which became the Union of French Indochina. Rice was abundant there and coal mines were developed. With the advent of the automobile in the twentieth century, the production of rubber enriched French planters.

Siam, squeezed between Burma and Indochina, remained nominally independent after giving up a large share of its territories and meeting other demands from Britain and France.

The lower part of the Malay Peninsula was organized into the Federated Malay States under the control or supervision of the British, who profited greatly from tin mining and rubber production.

Under an agreement with Great Britain, the Netherlands strengthened its grip over the Dutch East Indies, now called Indonesia. The land was endowed with petroleum as well as other minerals, timber, and agricultural resources.

The smaller islands of the southwestern Pacific, most of which had little commercial value, were useful as future naval bases. They were grabbed by countries with enough naval power to defend them. The British took the Fiji Islands and part of Samoa, and shared New Guinea with the Netherlands and Germany. The United States took part of the Samoan Islands; Germany took the Carolines, Marianas, and Marshalls; and France annexed Tahiti. The lesser islands were distributed among these major powers as well as Australia and New Zealand, members of the British Commonwealth.

AMERICA BECOMES
A POWER IN ASIA

Most Americans disapproved of European imperialism. Yet the United States had brought most of Latin America under the semicolonial umbrella of the Monroe Doctrine, had enjoyed the benefits of British and French colonial aggression in China, and in 1898 exploited the Spanish-American War as an opportunity to take control of Spain's remaining colonies in the Caribbean and the Pacific Ocean. While American troops were driving the Spaniards out of Cuba and Puerto Rico, the U.S. Asiatic Squadron attacked the Philippines, still a colony of Spain. In the brief Battle of Manila Bay, the squadron, commanded by Commodore George Dewey, destroyed Spain's fleet.

Having no land forces to capture Manila, Dewey enlisted the support of Emilio Aguinaldo, a patriot who had led an unsuccessful rebellion against Spain. Aguinaldo un-

*Americans guarding prisoners during
the Philippine uprising, 1900*

derstood that Dewey had promised independence for the Philippines in exchange for his help. In this belief, he organized a liberation army, defeated Spain, and declared the Philippines independent.

Dewey denied that he had promised independence and promptly took possession in the name of the United States. Spain then ceded the islands to the United States for $20 million, but Aguinaldo continued to fight for independence. After more than two years of brutal warfare, American troops crushed Aguinaldo's liberation forces. The Filipinos were again under colonial domination, although some of its worst features were tempered gradually by social reforms and partial self-government.

During the Spanish-American war, the United States also annexed Hawaii. The nominally independent government had already fallen under the control of scheming sugar planters and merchants from the U.S. mainland. Some Americans felt that their government had shown itself to be as greedy and domineering as the European colonialists. President William McKinley denied any imperial ambitions. "If we can benefit these remote peoples, who will object?" he asked. "If in the years of the future they are established in government under law and liberty, who will regret our perils and sacrifices? Who will not rejoice in our humanity?" But the so-called Land of the Free, now with Hawaii, Guam, Samoa, Wake Island, and the Philippines as stepping stones, was already striding boldly into the arena of Asian colonialism.

SLICING THE MELON

Japan's victory in the Sino-Japanese war made ambitious Western nations realize that they would have to move quickly or be denied their share of the spoils. Thus, as the United States was grabbing Hawaii and the Philippines, the European powers began "the slicing of the melon," as the conquest of China was called in the late nineteenth century.

In 1897, the Germans, latecomers like the Americans, occupied Kiaochow Bay and the seaport city of Tsingtao. In the following year China yielded to the British a privileged position in the Yangtze valley, the richest market in East Asia. China was also forced to open its extensive inland waterways to foreign steamers. This right helped the foreign powers to practice what had come to be known as "gunboat diplomacy." The Germans were given a ninety-nine-year lease on Kiaochow and the right to operate mines and build railways in Shantung Province. At almost the same time, Russia got a twenty-five-year lease on the Liaotung Peninsula, dominating the strategic Gulf of Chihli, and the right to build a railway across Manchuria. In 1898, France obtained a ninety-nine-year lease on Kwangchow Bay and the right to build a railway. The British then obtained a ninety-nine-year lease on Kowloon—part of their great commercial and naval center at Hong Kong —and the right to occupy Weihaiwei, across from Russia's Port Arthur.

The United States did not take part directly in this so-called scramble for concessions. But in 1899 Secretary of State John Hay proposed the Open Door policy under which powers with "spheres of influence" in China would agree to protect China's independence and assure equal treatment for all powers engaged in trade with China. This was intended mainly to protect future American interests against a European and Japanese monopoly of China trade. Since the other imperialist powers did not publicly reject this rather idealistic proposal, the United States assumed that it had been accepted. Although the principle was often invoked in later disputes, it did nothing to stop the plunder.

THE BOXER REBELLION

The "slicing of the melon" caused a violent reaction within China. Antiforeign sentiment came to a focus in the Society of Righteous Harmonious Fists, whose members were called "Boxers" because they practiced an exercise similar to shadow boxing. Members of this secret society opposed their government's yielding to foreign aggression. They also hated the Christian missionaries, who had swarmed into China under the unequal treaties and meddled in local religious affairs. The Boxers were ferocious fighters, made doubly fearless by a superstition that they could not be hurt by enemy bullets. In a widespread uprising, the Boxers burned Christian missions and killed many missionaries and Chinese converts in northern China.

The Boxers were at first determined to overthrow the government, but by various means they were won over to a pro-Manchu position by antiforeign elements in the court who secretly encouraged them to step up their attacks. In June 1900, as Boxer terrorism raged, foreign diplomats mobilized troops to defend their legations in the capital. As these troops marched toward Peking, foreign warships attacked forts near Tientsin. The Manchu court declared war. Imperial troops and Boxer guerrillas in Peking laid siege to the legation quarter, trapping nearly a thousand foreigners and a larger number of Chinese Christians who had sought refuge there. Meanwhile, the foreign powers were organizing a much larger expeditionary force of about 20,000 troops, mainly Japanese, British, Russian, American, and Chinese.

After several weeks, the expeditionary force reached Peking, routed the rebels, and lifted the siege of the legations. Most of the Manchu court fled; foreign troops again looted the city. The invaders ignored China's declaration of war in order to preserve the advantageous treaty system. However, foreigners doubled the number of their troops stationed in North China.

With the Manchu court at their mercy, further concessions were won. The Manchu government was saddled with an indemnity of more than $700 million, to be repaid over a period of forty years. Part of this staggering sum was to be raised from customs duties, but the victors had set the import tariff at the low rate of 5 percent.

This made it difficult for the Chinese to obtain revenue from trade. The remainder was to be raised by various internal revenues, including the tax on salt. This placed the burden of paying for the war on the very poor. China was required to destroy forts defending its coasts and waterways and to permit the stationing of foreign troops. Although the bankrupt Manchu court was restored to nominal power, China was now virtually an occupied country and remained so for nearly half a century.

THE RUSSO-JAPANESE WAR

Since the Sino-Japanese war and the Boxer incident, the Western powers had come to regard Japan as either a dangerous rival or a possible ally. Britain, with most of its troops tied down in the Boer War in South Africa, was greatly concerned over the aggressiveness of Russia. Taking advantage of the confusion attending the Boxer uprising, Russia had marched 100,000 troops into southern Manchuria and now threatened Britain's and Japan's spheres of interest. Both were more fearful because Russia had nearly completed the Trans-Siberian Railway and the Chinese Eastern Railway. Additionally, Russia was building a line across southern Manchuria to Port Arthur. From this point, Russia could easily stage attacks against adversaries in China proper. Because of this Russian threat, Great Britain and Japan signed a new treaty, the Anglo-Japanese Alliance, in 1902. This treaty was meant to protect Britain's privileged position in China and Japan's "special interest" in Korea. The signers also pledged mutual assistance in case of war.

Japan, now having the world's strongest sea power as an ally, immediately started preparations for war against the Russian Empire. In 1904, as a reaction to Russian interference in Korea, Japan's navy launched a surprise attack on Port Arthur, bottling up the Russian fleet, and war was declared. During two years of armed conflict, terribly costly in life and treasure for both sides, Japan defeated Russia. One of the greatest naval engagements in history climaxed the Russo-Japanese War. During the Battle of Tsushima in the Sea of Japan, Japan's navy annihilated the Russian fleet.

Most Americans applauded Japan's prowess and fighting spirit. The island kingdom had seemed at first to be striving against hopeless odds. American bankers had provided large loans to Japan during the war. Through the mediation of President Theodore Roosevelt, Japan's and Russia's peace missions met in New Hampshire and signed the Treaty of Portsmouth. This treaty recognized Japan's "paramount interest" in Korea, gave Japan Russia's lease on the Liaotung Peninsula, and ceded the lower half of Sakhalin, a large island north of Japan.

Under the treaty, Manchuria was to be returned to China. Both nations' troops were to be withdrawn. But Japan was permitted to take over Russia's lease on the railway zone in southern Manchuria and to station guards—actually soldiers—along the right of way extending from Harbin to Port Arthur. This concession enabled Japan to maintain an army in this territory, expand its economic influence, and eventually to capture all of southern Manchuria.

Now with a free hand in Korea, Japan tightened its grip on the country in an attempt to overcome bitter internal resistance to Japan's domination. In 1909 former prime minister Hirobumi Ito of Japan, who had ruled harshly as governor general of Korea, was assassinated by a Korean patriot. The following year, using this incident as a pretext, Japan annexed Korea by force. The grab was not opposed by governments in Europe or by the United States. Despite the Open Door policy, the United States gave its secret approval to the annexation in exchange for Japan's promise not to interfere in the Philippines.

Japan—the Land of the Rising Sun—with a stable government, vigorous industries, and a growing merchant fleet as well as powerful military and naval forces, at last could compete equally with Western imperialists.

CHAPTER 8
THE GATHERING STORM

Japan's victory over Russia had far-reaching consequences. For the first time in modern history an Asian people had defeated a major Western power. The victory gave other Asians confidence. In the decades that followed, nationalist movements in Asian colonies grew larger and stronger.

It should be remembered that the imperialists, to make their tasks of governing easier and less costly, had trained some native people to fill lower-ranking government and commercial positions. These better-educated people, together with merchants, doctors, lawyers, and others who had prospered under colonialism, formed a new middle class. Most of them were obedient to their foreign-controlled governments, but some joined movements demanding social reforms or even stirred up forcible resistance.

The national liberation movement was strongest in China. The most prominent leader of the movement was Sun Yat-sen, a Chinese Christian who had attended school in Honolulu and studied medicine in Hong Kong. Returning to China, he was deeply dissatisfied with conditions there. He vowed to overthrow the Manchu tyranny and began plotting against the government. To escape execution as a rebel, he fled the country in 1895, visiting Japan, the United States—where he became a citizen—and other countries. Among Chinese living outside their homeland, he organized an international campaign to make China free.

Among the Japanese, too, Dr. Sun and his followers found support. In Japan there were societies of nationalists who hoped to liberate all of Asia from Western imperial-

ism. Dreaming of an Asia for the Asians, they traveled widely and worked diligently to learn the languages, customs, and political conditions in the countries they hoped to bring under Japan's protection. Although these secret societies often used assassination and other criminal methods to accomplish their purposes, they were supported by the government. They acted as an unofficial intelligence agency to spearhead Japan's expansion in China.

The government's foreign policy was strongly influenced by several large companies, called *zaibatsu,* or money cliques. They dominated Japan's economy and led the country's advance into Manchuria and other parts of China by means of trade, shipping, railway building, and industrial development. In the early 1900s Japan was conducting normal relations with the Manchu rulers while at the same time some zaibatsu and government leaders—in league with the army and the secret societies—were scheming to topple the dynasty and replace it with a regime more friendly toward Japan. Dr. Sun, with a worldwide organization and strong support in China as well, suited their purpose. He was befriended and given money, weapons, and other assistance.

Also important for the liberation movement were Chinese students and teachers. After the Boxer uprising, the Manchu government had at last realized the need for modernization and had sent large numbers of educated youths abroad for further study. Many thousands of them flocked to Japan, attracted by its success in resisting imperialism and in developing its national power. Recruited in Japan by anti-Manchu leaders such as Dr. Sun, they returned to China and participated in movements to establish representative government.

The first revolution in China was launched in 1911. With Japan's help, the rebels set up a republican govern-

Sun Yat-sen

ment in Nanking, and the Manchu rulers were overthrown. Dr. Sun temporarily became China's first president.

In 1914, the First World War swept over Europe. Japan, still bound by the Anglo-Japanese Alliance, entered the war on the side of Britain, France, and Russia, who were pitted against Germany and Austria-Hungary, and the Ottoman Empire. As these nations girded for battle in Europe, Japan invaded China's rich province of Shantung, a German concession. At the same time, Japan's navy took possession of all the German-held islands in the western Pacific—the Marshalls, Marianas, and Carolines.

Having won these territories with little opposition, Japan put its mines, factories, and merchant fleet at the disposal of its allies. During four years of war which devastated and impoverished Europe, Japan doubled the tonnage of its merchant marine and quadrupled its industrial production. The war boom was especially profitable because Japan not only did almost none of the fighting but also captured Asian markets formerly monopolized by Europeans.

Pressing its advantage to the hilt, Japan presented China with a secret list of demands that would have made China almost a colony. Not all of them were granted, but in 1917 Peking was forced to yield a ninety-nine-year lease on Port Arthur and Dairen; commercial, railway-building, and mineral rights in Manchuria and Mongolia, and control of the most valuable coal and iron mines in China proper.

From the 1890s until the outbreak of the First World War, China had been sustained by huge loans from foreign powers. These were needed not only for modernizing industrial and transportation facilities, but also for repaying the principal and interest on previous debts. In time, payments on these debts consumed most of China's public revenue, and the government had to borrow more and more money abroad.

After World War I broke out, European nations had little money to lend to China. Japan's banks, on the other hand, were bulging with war profits. As a means of strengthening its hold on China, Japan advanced about $150 million to various public and private organizations in China. A large part of this sum, the so-called Nishihara loans, was given secretly to corrupt politicians as bribes. In return Japanese businessmen received further concessions.

In November 1918 the First World War ended in victory for the Allies. A peace conference began at Versailles, France, the following January. China, which had entered the war in support of the Allies, demanded that territories seized by Japan be returned. Japan, however, had already made agreements with its European allies and the United States that gave recognition of its "special interests" and territorial gains. As a result, Japan was permitted to keep control over Shantung and over the Pacific islands seized from Germany.

The Versailles decisions aroused strong resentment in China. University students organized mass protests against the Twenty-one Demands, the Nishihara Loans, and Japan's occupation of Shantung. Demonstrations swelled into a nationwide upsurge of anti-Japanese and anti-imperialist feeling.

CHAPTER 9
WINDS OF REVOLUTION

The First World War brought few changes to the colonies except to redistribute Germany's possessions among the victorious powers. However, one consequence of the war—the Russian Revolution—gave a tremendous push to Asian anti-imperialist forces. That revolution, in 1917, put an end to the old czarist Russian Empire and established the Union of Soviet Socialist Republics under a government based on the teachings of Karl Marx and Nikolai Lenin.

Unlike previous anticolonialists, the Communists believed that capitalism would have to be replaced by communism before the colonialists could be driven out. The Communist strategy was to organize peasants and workers —the majority of colonial peoples—for revolutionary struggles against their oppressors.

Many Communist-led liberation movements sprang up in Asia during the 1920s and 1930s. The Japanese, more ambitious than ever to control China, feared Communist gains in that country. They pinned their hopes on anti-Communist Nationalist government leader General Chiang Kai-shek, who had received his military education in Japan. Like his brother-in-law Dr. Sun Yat-sen, Chiang had many Japanese friends in high positions. But Chiang was unable to defeat the Communists or to control the warlords who ruled almost as dictators in several regions. Japan's very large investments in China, especially in southern Manchuria, were threatened both by Communist guerrilla attacks and by the treachery of warlords. Japan was worried too about the Nationalist government's policy of encouraging Chinese competition against Japanese-controlled railways and other monopolies.

Japan was in a difficult position. By letting the situation go from bad to worse, it might lose its precious interests in China. But if it invaded China to protect those interests, the act would antagonize the United States and Great Britain, both important business partners. By 1930, however, there was not much friendship to lose. Since the end of World War I, Western admiration for Japan had become clouded with mistrust. Sensational newspaper stories in the United States and Europe screamed warnings against the "Yellow Peril" that threatened the "white race." In the United States laws were passed against the immigration of Orientals.

In 1921, at an international naval conference in Washington, D.C., Japan had been forced to accept a position inferior to that of the United States and Great Britain in regard to the size of its navy. Japan had already been forced to give up Shantung and other valuable concessions in China. When the naval inequality was upheld in a second treaty, signed in London in 1930, there was great indignation in Japan. This ill feeling was directed against the civilian government which accepted the treaty. The public outrage was exploited by military expansionists, who were gaining control of the nation.

Japan's situation was made worse by the worldwide depression that began around 1930. Demand for Japan's exports shrank. The nation tried to solve the problem by producing cheaper goods. Foreign countries, faced with similar economic problems, set up trade barriers against those goods, and Japan's depression deepened. The militarists told the people that if Japan could get a more secure hold on the markets and raw materials of the China mainland, the nation's economic troubles would be solved. There was a great public outcry for territorial expansion.

Voices of moderation argued that the conquest of China should be gradual. Patriotic expansionists spoke more loudly, demanding the protection of Japan's so-

called rights in China. In 1931 Japan's army settled the debate by suddenly taking over the huge territory of southern Manchuria. The imperial government explained to the world that the move had been made in self-defense. A new "nation," Manchukuo, was set up under a puppet government controlled from Tokyo.

This aggression was little different from past actions of other imperialists. Nevertheless, it alarmed some countries that wanted the Open Door to China's market. The takeover also violated the rules of the League of Nations—established after World War I to prevent the use of force in settling international disputes. When the aggression in Manchuria was condemned by other league members, Japan walked out. The island nation became a lone wolf in an increasingly hostile world.

Generalissimo Chiang Kai-shek and Lieutenant General Joseph Stilwell. Known as Vinegar Joe, Stilwell was sent to oversee setting up air bases, supply depots, and the training of Chinese soldiers.

CHAPTER 10
THE SHOWDOWN

Japan resolved to make all of China its colony. The first decisive move was made in 1937, after a minor skirmish between Japanese and Chinese troops near Peking. Japan used the incident as an excuse for pouring more troops into China, and in a short time Peking and other major cities were occupied.

Atrocities against Chinese civilians shocked the world, but Japan seemed no longer to care about public opinion and even dared to bomb British and American gunboats in the Yangtze River.

As Japan had anticipated, Great Britain and France —already facing the prospect of another war against Germany—were reluctant to risk hostilities with Japan. The United States, bound by an official policy of neutrality, did not then intervene either. Nevertheless, the conquest of China proved more difficult than Japan had expected.

Japan, fighting what it called a "holy war against Communism," found itself bogged down year after year in the vast peasant-populated interior of China, but did not give up. Japan's military leaders believed that if they could control the resources of Southeast Asia they could not only win the war against China but defeat the Western powers too if the need arose.

The outbreak of the Second World War in Europe, in September 1939, made it impossible for Britain, France, and the Netherlands to defend their colonies in Asia. Japan took this opportunity to proclaim the Greater East Asia Coprosperity Sphere. It included all the colonial regions of

*Japan's troops fighting in
the Chinese city of Shanghai*

the Far East. Hoping to strengthen its international position, Japan signed a mutual assistance treaty with Germany and Italy, the so-called Axis powers. To protect its northern flank, Japan signed a nonaggression pact with the Soviet Union.

Thus prepared, Japan's forces moved into French Indochina under an arrangement with the government of German-occupied France. Responding to this threat against Southeast Asia, President Franklin D. Roosevelt warned Japan that its aggression would force him to take drastic measures to safeguard American interests in Asia.

Japan's Prime Minister Hideki Tojo paid no attention to this warning. He was already planning to drive all other imperialist powers out of the Far East. There was one big obstacle to Japan's ambitions. The United States, Great Britain, and the Netherlands had imposed a total embargo on exports to Japan. This meant, for one thing, that Japan's petroleum supplies, absolutely necessary for waging modern war, were being cut to a trickle. Japan had barely enough oil in reserve to fight for two years.

The American terms for ending the embargo were that Japan must remove its armed forces from Indochina and China, including Manchuria. This would have deprived Japan of all territorial gains won during the previous ten years. Japan continued to negotiate with the United States for more acceptable terms. All the while its oil supplies were draining away. Japan's military leaders decided that the only way to win a war against the West was to begin it immediately.

On December 7, 1941, Japan bombed Hawaii, the Philippines, Hong Kong, and Malaya. In a series of stunning naval victories the small island nation quickly became master of the western Pacific. Japan occupied East and Southeast Asia from Korea and Manchuria to Burma, the Dutch East Indies, the Celebes, part of New Guinea, and many smaller islands of the Pacific. The Greater East Asia Coprosperity Sphere was the largest colonial empire since the days of the Spanish and Portuguese conquerors.

Japan had made long and careful preparations for this achievement by cultivating the friendship of political leaders in the region. Thus, friendly or at least obedient governments existed or were set up in most of the invaded countries. Japan won the cooperation of colonial peoples by promises of liberation from foreign domination. But in some countries, notably Indochina, Malaya, Burma, and the Philippines, native peoples organized underground movements and waged guerrilla warfare against the Japanese "liberators."

By 1944, the Allies had stopped Hitler's advance in Europe. The United States began an all-out naval and air assault on Japan's empire. Allied submarines and aircraft sank most of Japan's merchant vessels and warships. Japan did not have enough gasoline to fuel its planes to stop the rapidly approaching enemy. The United States and allied forces captured Japan's far-flung island bases one after another. Japan's major cities and industrial centers of the home islands were not spared. Bombings from the air destroyed large areas.

On August 6, 1945, the United States dropped an atomic bomb, the first ever used in warfare, on the city of Hiroshima in western Japan. Two days later the Soviet Red Army invaded Manchuria and soon defeated Japan's forces there. On August 9 another atomic bomb destroyed most of another city, Nagasaki. On the fifteenth Japan surrendered.

Japan was occupied by United States troops commanded by General Douglas MacArthur. His first task was to break up Japan's overseas empire. The British, French, and Dutch colonies were immediately reclaimed by their former owners. Japan's colony of Formosa and its puppet states on the mainland were returned to China. Korea regained its independence. The Soviet Union got the Kurile Islands and southern Sakhalin. The Pacific islands that Japan had seized from Germany in 1914 were placed under the protection of the United States, which had already recovered the Philippines as well as Guam, Wake, and

The city of Hiroshima, Japan,
after the United States
dropped the atomic bomb

Midway islands. The Ryukyu Islands, part of Japan, were placed under direct U.S. administration. Japan's far-flung empire was thus stripped down to its four main islands—Hokkaido, Honshu, Shikoku, and Kyushu—and nearby smaller islands. The total area was about the size of California. All Japanese military and civilian personnel in the Greater East Asia Coprosperity Sphere were sent home to Japan.

The nation remained under U.S. occupation until a peace treaty took effect in 1952. Under the occupation Japan was completely disarmed and given a democratic constitution that prohibited the possession or use of military forces. The Asian colonial structure had returned to normal. Or so it may have seemed to Western optimists. But during the war, the world had undergone changes that could never be reversed.

CHAPTER 11
A NEW WORLD ORDER?

Japan's purpose in waging war against the Western powers was to make their colonies part of its own empire. By an unexpected turn of events the effect of the war was to liberate those colonies and put an end to the age of imperialism. While the imperialists were busy fighting each other, colonial peoples got a brief taste of freedom from their Western conquerors. At the same time they found that an Asian dominator was no more agreeable. Many colonial men and women learned the arts of underground warfare while resisting Japan.

Even before Japan started the war in the Pacific, the Western imperialists had found it necessary to promise their colonies future freedom. In August 1941, when the British and their European allies were fighting for survival against Hitler's Germany, Prime Minister Winston Churchill and President Roosevelt met at sea and issued the Atlantic Charter, a declaration of principles intended for winning the allegiance of other countries, including the colonies.

The charter promised to restore sovereign rights to peoples who had been deprived of them and to ensure all nations equal access to the world's trade and raw materials. The charter held out hope for improved labor conditions, economic progress, and security. It promised freedom of the seas and freedom from fear and want in all lands. The use of force to settle international disputes was forbidden, and aggressors were to be disarmed. These principles became part of the United Nations Charter, which laid the foundation for the United Nations Organization established in 1945.

This global declaration of independence was a very curious document to have been composed and accepted by the same powers that had previously divided East Asia among themselves with little regard for the rights of the conquered peoples. Indeed, as soon as the war was over, the European powers tried their best to recapture their Asian colonies rather than liberate them. The economic needs that led the European nations toward Asia in the past had become even sharper in the middle of the twentieth century.

The world had changed, however. The earlier success of the colonizers had been based upon superior power. But by 1945 the European countries were exhausted by the global conflict while Asian liberation forces had become stronger and more confident. Thus, the UN Charter, or parts of it, became a reality in Asia. The captive countries won independence one after another. Within ten years or so, only a few fragments of foreign empire remained.

Although the pace of liberation was swift, the breakup of colonial empires was no less bloody and bitter than their beginnings. The first great upheaval occurred in India. Nationalist leaders had offered to support Great Britain's war effort only in exchange for full independence. The British rulers resisted this demand. Protest demonstrations, strikes, and religious riots that paralyzed India followed. Mahatma Gandhi led enormous civil disobedience campaigns. Mohammed Ali Jinnah clamored for the establishment of a separate Muslim state. The Communists, who had gained control over organized labor, raised the threat of revolution. Britain, finding its position impossible, at last granted independence in 1947. Two independent nations, India and Pakistan—headed by Jawaharlal Nehru and Mohammed Ali Jinnah respectively—were established within the British Commonwealth. Ceylon and Burma gained independence the following year.

Other Asian colonies were eager to follow India's example. In fact, some had issued declarations of independence immediately after the war. However, the pace slowed when the capitalist and Communist countries began a "cold war" for world supremacy. The former colonies became part of the stakes in a mammoth game of power. It was apparent that Communist parties, closely linked with those of Russia and China, were gaining strength all over Asia, including U.S.-occupied Japan. The United States and the old colonial powers feared that newly independent countries would be taken over by Communists, thereby strengthening the so-called red bloc.

The UN had been set up to keep peace and guarantee the right of nations to choose their own forms of government without interference. It turned out that the imperialist powers, who dominated the world organization, were more interested in suppressing revolutionary movements than in defending a nation's right to choose.

At first, the Americans upheld the principles of the UN Charter. The United States granted partial independence to the Philippines, America's only Asian colony, in 1946. Then U.S. policy changed. America—whose policy had once been to avoid foreign entanglements—took on the responsibility of policing the entire "free world," a term loosely applied to the non-Communist countries.

This decision put the democratic United States in the odd position of helping governments that were trying to restore colonialism by force. Thus, the Netherlands was helped financially in its efforts to reconquer the East Indies. France received substantial aid for retaking Indochina, and Britain for holding on to Malaya. The United States put up huge amounts of cash and weapons to support China's Nationalists against the Communists. None of these campaigns succeeded.

United States efforts to isolate China, after the Communist victory there in 1949, involved America in two major Asian wars—in Korea (1950–53) and in Vietnam (1945–75). The latter was part of the larger Indochina conflict, and perhaps could be called the last great war to

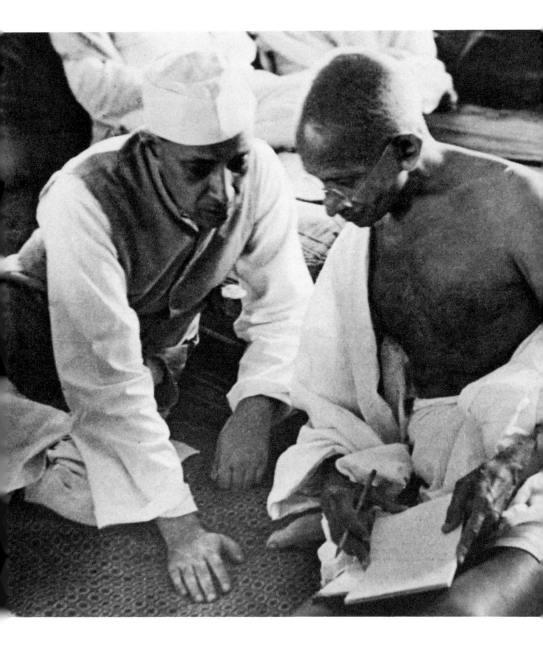

Mahatma Gandhi, right,
and *Jawaharlal Nehru*

preserve colonialism. The Indochina war caused enormous devastation and suffering and resulted in the deaths of an estimated 3,200,000 people. More than 2,500,000 Americans served in Indochina, mainly in Vietnam, and 56,000 of them were killed. The United States spent as much as $200 billion on the war, in addition to billions given to France before its defeat by the Vietnamese in 1954.

In addition to the wars in Korea and Vietnam there were at least a dozen others in Asia after 1945. Those wars involved India, Pakistan, Bangladesh, Burma, Indonesia, China, Taiwan, and nearly every other country or colony in Asia. The conflicts were of various origins, but most were direct or indirect consequences of colonialism. In some cases, old hatreds aggravated by colonial rulers were to blame. In others, former subject peoples were pitted against each other on the old principle of divide and conquer. Some were provoked by Communist revolutionaries carrying the anticolonial struggle to its climax, or by anti-Communists struggling to preserve capitalist privileges. Almost without exception the funds and equipment were supplied by outsiders, mainly the United States and the Soviet Union. Both of these superpowers claimed to be promoting the freedom and welfare of the countries they were assisting.

At any rate, very few East Asian countries—whether Communist, anti-Communist, or neutral—are either free or prosperous. The Communist governments enforce strict discipline and regulate most aspects of social and economic life. Most of the non-Communist countries are ruled by dictatorships supported by economic and military aid provided by foreign governments. In the latter countries, especially those in Southeast Asia, much of the natural wealth and commerce are exploited by large international corporations as in the days of the East India companies.

These corporations, overwhelmingly American, exert tremendous influence upon the countries in which they operate. This form of economic and political domination is sometimes called neocolonialism.

As in the past, one of the main attractions of Asia is an abundance of cheap labor that can be employed profitably by foreign investors. Most of the Asian countries that were geared to the colonial system are still weak and backward economically. Drained of their wealth for centuries, they have too little capital for development. Their governments are heavily burdened with debts to foreign banks.

There are significant exceptions. Japan, with American help, has managed to build the third largest economy in the world. Both North and South Korea, as well as Taiwan, Malaysia, Singapore, and the British colony of Hong Kong, have made considerable progress economically. A few other Southeast Asian nations are following their example. The people of mainland China are still quite poor according to world standards. Yet for the first time in modern history they—now numbering more than 800 million—are leading lives free from the famines, floods, and epidemics that once ravaged their country.

Generally speaking, the nations of Asia must be included among the so-called developing countries of the world. These are mainly former colonies afflicted by mass poverty made worse by high birth rates. Although these countries contain 70 percent of the world's population, they earn less than one-third of its income. In the "developing" countries of Asia alone (with about one-fourth of the world's population) the income per person is only about $50 a year, as compared with $3,000 in Japan and $6,600 in the United States. Furthermore, the economic gap between the former colonies and the industrial countries is becoming wider.

These grim facts have been recognized by many world leaders. For example, a few years ago Pope Paul VI declared: "Politically and economically weak nations are being held by others in a state of quasi slavery. There are examples of continuous subjection by colonial powers. There are cases of more or less explicit neocolonialism. . . ."

The liberated colonies are by no means resigned to such a fate. Nor are they content to be part of the power struggle between the capitalist and Communist powers. In 1950, the prime ministers of India and China jointly called for the peaceful coexistence of nations and the formation of an association of countries aligned with neither side in the cold war. The subsequent Bandung Conference, held in Indonesia, marked the birth of the Third World. This loose group of African and Asian nations resolved to remain outside the blocs led by the capitalist and Communist superpowers. That was in 1955, and in the years that followed, the nonaligned or neutral countries have been assuming a more and more important role in world affairs.

In 1960, the United Nations General Assembly issued a declaration of independence for colonial countries and peoples, and formed the Special Committee on Colonialism to handle the problems of dependent areas. This trend reflected the fact that the newly independent countries were growing rapidly in number and eventually gained a majority position in the assembly.

In 1974 the General Assembly affirmed that the developing countries would stand together against foreign exploitation of their resources, and issued a "Declaration on the Establishment of a New International Economic Order," which stated in part: ". . . the remaining vestiges of alien and colonial domination, foreign occupation, racial discrimination, apartheid and neocolonialism in all its forms continue to be among the greatest obstacles to the full emancipation and progress of the developing countries and all the peoples involved. . . ."

As a basis for correcting these injustices, the declaration called for the total equality of states, the self-determination of peoples, and the prohibition of territorial aggression. It called for participation of all countries on an equal basis in solving world economic problems and absolute control of all nations over their natural resources and economic activities.

INDEX

French East India Co., 18
French Indochina, Union of,
  51

Gandhi, Mahatma, 75
General Assembly, declaration of 1974, 81
Genghis Khan, 4–8
Germany, 2, 26, 47, 49, 50,
  52, 55, 62, 63, 64, 74
    in World War II, 68–73
Goa, 16, 29
Gobi Desert, 7
Good Hope, Cape of, 10
Government of India Act, 23,
  25
Great Britain, 18
    See also England
Great Wall, 4, 7
Greater East Asia Coprosperity Sphere, 68, 70, 73
Greece, ancient, 3
Greeks, ancient, 1
Guam, 54, 71

Harbin, 58
Harris, Townsend, 44
Hawaii, 54, 70
Hay, John, 55
Hinduism. See Religion
Hindus. See India
Hiroshima, 71
Hitler, Adolf, 71, 74
Hokkaido, 73
Holy Roman Empire, 12, 13
Hong Kong, 12, 35, 39, 55,
  59, 70, 79
Honshu, 73

Hungary, 4

Imperialism, 2
  Age of, 51–63
  See also Colonialism;
    individual countries
India, 1, 3, 4, 7, 10, 13–25,
  31, 32, 33, 75, 76, 78, 81
Indian Ocean, 10, 12
Indochina, 70, 71, 76, 78
Indonesia, 2, 52, 78, 81
Industrial development, 1, 2
  in Japan, 40–50
Industrial Revolution, 26, 28
Inventions, in Asia, 1
Islam. See Religion
Italy, 70
Ito, Hirobumi, 46, 58

Jahan, 17, 18
Jahangir, 17
Japan, 3, 12, 15, 29, 55, 57–
  63, 64–66, 74, 76, 79
    industrial development
      in, 40–50
    in World War II, 68–73
Japanese archipelago, 2
Java, 15, 29
Jinnah, Mohammed Ali, 75

Kiaochow Bay, 55
Korea, 4, 49, 50, 57, 58, 70,
  71, 76, 78, 79
Korean Peninsula, 2
Kowloon Peninsula, 36, 55
Kublai Khan, 4, 7
Kurile Islands, 71
Kwangchow Bay, 55

Tientsin, 36, 56
Taj Mahal, 17
Tamerlane, 4, 7, 17
Taoism, 3
Tartars. *See* Mongols
Thailand, 2
Third World, 81
Timor, 16, 29
Tojo, Hideki, 70
Tokyo, 44, 46, 66
Tonkin, 51
Trade, 26–39, 40–50
Trans-Siberian Railway, 57
Triple Intervention (Japan), 50
Tsingtao, 55
Tsushima, Battle of, 58
Turkistan, 4

USSR, 64
    See also Russia
United Nations, 75, 76, 81
United States, 2, 26, 65, 74, 76, 78, 79
    and Japan, 40–50
    power in Asia, 52–54, 59–63

in World War II, 68–73
United States Asiatic Squadron, 52

Venice, 7, 9, 12
Versailles, 63
Victoria, Queen, 25
Vietnam, 2, 51, 76, 78
Vladivostok, 39

Wake Island, 54, 71
Wars, after World War II, 74–81
Weihaiwei, 55
World War I, 62, 63, 64, 65, 66
World War II, 2, 68–73

Xanadu, 7

Yangtze River and Valley, 55, 68
"Yellow Peril," 65
Yellow River, 7
Yokohama, 44